D1389834

the art of
Positive
Living

how to see the good
in everyday life

An Hachette UK Company
www.hachette.co.uk

First published in Great Britain in 2021 by Pyramid,
an imprint of Octopus Publishing Group Ltd.
Carmelite House
50 Victoria Embankment
London, EC4Y 0DZ
www.octopusbooks.co.uk

Distributed in the US by
Hachette Book Group
1290 Avenue of the Americas
4th and 5th Floors
New York, NY 10104

Distributed in Canada by
Canadian Manda Group
664 Annette St.
Toronto, Ontario, Canada M6S 2C8

ISBN: 978-0-7537-3471-1

A CIP catalogue record for this book is available from the British Library

Printed and bound in China

10 9 8 7 6 5 4 3 2 1

Publisher: Lucy Pessell
Designer: Hannah Coughlin
Junior Editor: Sarah Kennedy
Editorial Assistant: Emily Martin
Production Controllers: Nic Jones and Lucy Carter

the art of
Positive
Living

how to see the good
in everyday life

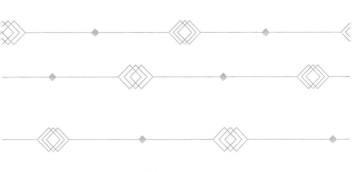

introduction

Being positive increases self-confidence, helps us to be more open to new experiences, enhances our joy, and keeps us energized and focused on our goals. With a positive outlook we can align with our true selves and attract wonderful things and people into our lives.

That isn't to say that positivity is about ignoring the problems and sadness in your life. Whether it's illness, losing a loved one, break-ups, job redundancy or stress and anxiety, there will always be parts of life that can sometimes feel impossible to overcome. And the added layer of social issues we are currently faced with – social media overload, political unrest, the threat of climate change, to name just a few – only serve to exacerbate negative thinking. Positivity is not about denying the existence of these bad parts of life; rather it's about choosing to see the good and remaining hopeful when times are tough.

The aim of this book is to inspire you to lead a life of positivity and optimism – to pick yourself up when you're down and to live a happier life. In these pages you'll find a wide range of tips for being more positive, from balancing your home and work life to seeing the bigger picture and practicing gratitude. Each tip is also accompanied by a quote to encourage you to see the glint of silver lining however dark the storm clouds may be. Don't let negativity drown out the song of your soul.

As you work through these pages, you may find there are some tips that work better than others for you – and that's okay. The road to living a more positive life will be different for everyone, and what matters most is that you achieve it in a way that feels right for you. Some key questions to ask yourself on your journey to positivity include things like 'What makes you truly happy?', 'What gives your life meaning?', 'What are your goals in life?'. Asking yourself these types of questions is the first step in changing your attitude, and you will find that, once you have the answers, positive thinking will start to come naturally.

how to use this book

In reading this book, follow your nose and see what speaks to you and what doesn't. Feel free to read this book from front to back, back to front, or simply to open a page every day to see what jumps out at you. If possible, start a journal to keep track of the actions you take and any insights that you have about yourself or your lifestyle. List resources that you find on your own. Keep track of improvements in your sense of well-being and overall happiness. Note any difficulties and resistance that you may be experiencing and try to explore the causes. Take your time and go slowly; shifting your negative thoughts to positive ones doesn't happen overnight, and it may take some practice before it starts to come naturally.

Don't forget to share the tips and tricks in this book with your friends and family. Positivity is contagious, and if the people around you start practicing positivity, it will become that bit easier for you to maintain in your everyday life.

put a positive spin
on your daily tasks

Those who wish to sing, always find a song.

Swedish proverb

Instead of feeling stressed by "having" to do certain things, switch your mindset to one of gratitude for being able to do them.

I "have" to pick up the kids from school becomes I "get" to pick up the kids from school; I "have" to clean the house becomes, "how lucky I am to have a house to clean"; I "have" to go to my exercise class becomes "I'm grateful for a healthy body that enables me to exercise", and so on.

It's amazing how quickly this lifts the weight of mundane or difficult chores and challenges.

make meditation a habit

Inspiration comes from within yourself. One has to be positive. When you're positive, good things happen.

Deep Roy, actor, stuntman and puppeteer

Meditation can alter your psychology, reprogramming the mind to be more positive, more grateful, and more adept at handling stress.

To explore and fully enjoy all of its benefits, consistency is key, so try to make it a daily habit. Pick a time you can commit to every day and carve out space where you can be free from clutter and other distractions.

9

learn something new

Anything's possible if you've got enough nerve.

J. K. Rowling, writer

Psychological research increasingly suggests that growth occurs at the edge of our comfort zone. So get uncomfortable and become a beginner again.

You don't necessarily have to parachute out of a plane but you can recharge your life and bring in positive energy by learning a new skill – this could be anything from mastering a musical instrument to trying a new recipe.

Open your mind to new experiences, be open to meeting new people, and making new friends. Take others' opinions on board. Open your heart to loved ones.

create positivity prompts

If you are positive, you'll see opportunities instead
of obstacles.

Widad Akrawi, human rights activist

Create your own personal symbols of hope. Designating
an object as a symbol of hope is a great way to remind
yourself there is life beyond whatever difficulties you are
experiencing right now. Perhaps it's a feather, a gemstone,
artwork you love, handmade trinkets from a child, or
photos of your family – anything that makes you smile or
reminds you of happy times. These will prompt your mind
to switch into a positive mode.

Whatever your chosen symbolic items, make sure
they're positioned somewhere you will see them often,
and when your eyes land on them, let it be a reminder
to remain hopeful.

turn setbacks around

Oh, my friend, it's not what they take away from you that counts. It's what you do with what you have left.

Hubert Humphrey, politician

When it comes to chasing dreams, be realistic and recognize that you will most likely face obstacles along the way. Acknowledging this and planning for any setbacks means that when they happen they won't knock you off course. You can just calmly put your plans for overcoming them into action.

If things go wrong, look at the lessons you have learned and all the ways in which these can help you move forward with a greater chance of success.

Living in the past and dwelling on previous mistakes will only serve to hinder your progress. Today, make the decision to forgive yourself for all of your past failings. You will walk lighter and feel braver and more positive if you can do this.

cherish your breath

Remember to breathe. It is, after all, the secret of life.

Gregory Maguire, writer

Even when it feels as though things around you are falling apart, you will always have your breath as a tool to centre yourself, calm the mind, and thereby switch your thinking patterns into something less destructive.

Simply breathe in slowly and deeply through your nose. Draw in the air and feel it fill your lungs. Now exhale slowly through your mouth.

This will have an immediate calming effect, both physiologically – deep breathing triggers our parasympathetic nervous system which controls our fight or flight response – and psychologically. Do this throughout the day, whenever you need to quell your nerves to face your fears.

look upwards and outwards

To the mind that is still, the whole universe surrenders.

Lao Tzu, philosopher

When we get wrapped up in ourselves it is very easy to lose perspective. Take some time out to remind yourself what a tiny part of the universe you are. Look up into a clear night's sky and gaze at the stars, or meditate on images of vast landscapes and take a moment to reflect on the world as a whole, and all the other people under this vast sky.

Reminding yourself of the size and scope of the universe does wonders for your perspective. So what if you forget a few of your words when speaking in public, or if you get turned down for promotion/a business loan/a date ... ? The world will still keep turning. Such thoughts may just give you the courage to try.

don't let labels define you

Love yourself. It is important to stay positive because beauty comes from the inside out.

Jenn Proske, actress

You're not your job, where you come from, or how much money you have. You are a unique individual and you do not have to conform to others' expectations of you.

smile more

Let your smile change the world, but don't let the world change your smile.

Connor Franta, entrepreneur, entertainer, and writer

Smile at your loved ones, at strangers in the street, at the person who served you coffee or cut your hair. Those smiles will be reflected right back at you, instantly improving your mood and outlook on the day.

If you're having a low moment and can't think of anything to smile about, you can trick your mind into feeling more positive simply through curling up the corners of your mouth.

check your attitude

A positive attitude causes a chain reaction of positive
thoughts, events and outcomes. It is a catalyst and it sparks
extraordinary results.

Wade Boggs, baseball player

Think of life as an echo – whatever you put out in the
world will be reflected back at you. If you have a negative
attitude and dish out angry words, the chances are you'll
end up being on the receiving end of similar behaviours.
On the other hand, project love and kindness out into the
world and that's what you'll receive.

Negativity inhibits us in so many ways, holding us
back from accomplishing our goals, damaging our self-
confidence and feelings of self-worth. Today, every time a
negative thought comes into your head, check yourself and
replace it with a positive one. This is much easier than it
sounds and you'll be amazed at the results!

set achievable goals

Instead of worrying about what you cannot control, shift your
energy to what you can create.

Roy T. Bennett, writer and motivational speaker

Ensure that your goals are attainable in order to retain
an optimistic outlook. If your aims are unrealistic and
unlikely to ever be achieved, you'll be constantly battling
with negative feelings about your life and feel angry with
yourself for not having completed them.

Set yourself a very attainable goal. Write down seven things
you can do in the next seven days to move you towards
your goal. Do this each and every week.

Once you have accomplished this, tick it off your list
and set to work on a new goal. Keep going in this way,
setting and achieving small goals. It's a great way to build
up your confidence, setting you up to tackle ever more
challenging tasks.

find a new perspective

One's destination is never a place, but a new way of
seeing things.

Henry Miller, writer

We're often our own worst critics, much harsher on
ourselves than we would be on others in the same
situation. So take a step back and look at your scenario
from a new perspective. Imagine you are listening to a
good friend telling you about their goal.

Would you focus on the pitfalls and "what ifs", or would
you simply admire them for their strength and courage, pat
them on the back and congratulate them for taking the risk?

crush negative self-talk

Keep your face to the sunshine and you cannot see a shadow.

Helen Keller, political activist

You know that little voice in your head that berates you for having got something wrong, or for not being good enough? Silence it. You can envisage literally replying to the voice with counter arguments as to why you are in fact perfectly capable, lovely, or simply good enough.

Identify the negative beliefs you hold about yourself and find counter arguments to challenge these. Find evidence where you have acted in a way, displayed behaviour or developed habits that contradict these negative ideas surrounding your sense of self.

This will help you to realize that much of your sense of self-worth comes from unfounded perceptions rather than reality.

keep a "gratitude" journal

When you think positive, good things happen.

Matt Kemp, baseball player

Do not indulge in self-pity. Wallowing in thoughts of all that may not be right with your life will leave you demotivated and caught up in a spiral of negativity. Instead, focus on all that you have.

Keep a gratitude journal and each night before you go to bed, write down three things for which you are grateful. This could be your family, your friends, the sound of birdsong in the air, or the sun on your face. Anything – big or small – for which you wish to give thanks.

Focusing on all that you have, as opposed to what you are lacking, will encourage the positive mindset required to make healthy, positive decisions.

find the humour

Life is 10 percent what happens to us and 90 percent how we react to it.

Dennis P. Kimbro, motivational speaker

Can you find the funny side of a bad situation? There's usually some humour to be found in even the darkest corners. If you can seek this out, it will help carry you through the tough days.

Learning to laugh at yourself can be a very positive experience. Even when you feel as though you're failing, find a way to take a step back and laugh kindly and gently at yourself.

Laughter improves health, mood, and social skills and is now even used as a therapy (laughter yoga was started in Mumbai by Dr. Madan Katarina, who is now happily running over 5,000 clubs worldwide). So raise those endorphin levels and have a good chuckle. Forcing a laugh can trick the body and mind into believing it's happy so even if you can't think of something to laugh about, just laugh and you'll soon find yourself in a happier and more positive mood.

don't be afraid of fear

Being scared is part of being alive. Accept it. Walk through it.

Robin S. Sharma, writer

Sometimes fear can be helpful – as humans we're wired towards self-preservation and the primal, instinctive response of fear can get us out of dangerous situations. However, in many day-to-day scenarios fear is far from helpful and if we respond to every fearful situation as if we're in mortal danger, i.e. we run a mile, we are unlikely to ever take risks and grow. So when you feel the fear, ask yourself if there is a real threat, or if the threat is simply to your ego or sense of comfort.

If the thing you fear is fear itself you will never find the motivation to pursue your dreams. Instead, you will get stuck in a self-perpetuating cycle of inaction and negativity. Often we want fear to go away before we take action. However, that's not how it works – fear doesn't just disappear. You have to swat it away or plow through it, circle around it ... In other words you move ahead in spite of it.

keep a "bravery" journal

As long as you feel pain, you're still alive. As long as you make mistakes, you're still human. And as long as you keep trying, there's still hope.

Susan Gale, writer

Try to develop awareness each time you do something you're scared of. You may well embark on positive and courageous acts every day of your life without really noticing. This is particularly true if you're shy. Maybe you've had to stand up and give a presentation, speak out in a meeting, ask a stranger for directions ...

Start a journal and each night write down something you did that day that made you feel uncomfortable. Acknowledging these acts of courage, however small, will boost your confidence and encourage you to keep being positive.

make a start

Either you run the day, or the day runs you.

Jim Rohn, motivational speaker

Whatever it is you want to do, whatever fears are holding you back, whatever excuses you've been giving yourself, do one thing today that takes a step towards your goal.

Stop waiting until you're 100 percent ready to embark on your project or goal. This will never, ever happen. There will always be elements – emotional, financial, practical, hypothetical – that will hold you back. If you wait until your situation is perfect you will be waiting forever. Don't hesitate, just go for it!

move mindfully
through your day

Look at the sparrows; they do not know what they will
do in the next moment. Let us literally live from moment
to moment.

Mahatma Gandhi, political ethicist

Try to walk deliberately and mindfully. Take slow steps and
notice your heartbeat, the sensation of material on your
skin, the quality of the air in the room.

Listen to the sound of your footsteps, to the birds singing,
to the sound of voices around you.

Notice what you are passing – the architecture of buildings,
the arch of a doorway, the colours and shapes of the plants.

26   Reconnecting with the moment can have a positive effect
on your entire day.

stay centred

Anywhere is paradise; it's up to you.

Unknown

Retreat to your centre in times of need to find strength
and encouragement. How do you find your centre? Ask
yourself what you love in this world more than yourself,
more than life itself. That's where your core being lies.

Staying centered throughout the day will help to prevent
you from being derailed by negative circumstances or
people you encounter. Find your centre each morning
before you leave the house through breathing techniques,
yoga, or any other activity that puts your mind at rest.

27

take a social media break

Look up, laugh loud, talk big, keep the colour in your cheek
and the fire in your eye, adorn your person, maintain your
health, your beauty and your animal spirits.

William Hazlitt, social commentator and philosopher

Nothing good can come of chasing "likes" and comparing
yourself to other people's curated visions of their life.
Take a week's break from social media and notice how this
impacts your mood.

do what you love

Sometimes you just have to turn the page to realize there's
more to your book of life than the page you're stuck on.

Trent Shelton, American football player

Is there a way to make your work align with your passions?
Can you turn hobbies or callings from the soul into ways
to make a living? Doing something you love every day can
help you live a truly fulfilled life.

keep a "that went well" journal

You cannot have a positive life and a negative mind.

Joyce Meyer, author and speaker

When you need to cultivate positivity it can be incredibly helpful to look back on past achievements. Designate a special place in which you record and store your proudest moments. This could be a scrapbook, a photo album or a notice board. Stick in/put up certificates, photos, letters, emails…whatever it is that serves as an instant reminder of what you have achieved. Looking through these things will boost your self-confidence and provide valuable motivation.

Keep a bedside journal, too. Before you go to bed each night, write down three things that went well for you that day, however insignificant they may seem. Then next to each of these things, note down why it happened – this will help you to recognize the behaviours and patterns that lead to positive outcomes.

practise self-compassion

Make sure your worst enemy doesn't live between your own two ears.

Laird Hamilton, big wave surfer

Treat yourself as you would a good friend. Often we treat ourselves in a manner in which we wouldn't dream of treating anyone else; we are harsher, more unforgiving, and frequently unkind. Step back and find ways in which to nurture yourself instead.

surround yourself
with positivity

Positive thinking is more than just a tagline. It changes the way we behave. And I firmly believe that when I am positive, it not only makes me better, but it also makes those around me better."

Harvey Mackay, businessman and author

Spend time with positive friends, family members, or co-workers and their attitude will rub off on you. Positivity is contagious!

Surround yourself with positive people who believe in you. Developing a positive outlook requires a certain level of self-esteem, so choose your friends wisely and only engage with people who boost your confidence and urge you to follow your dreams.

focus on solutions

If you don't like something change it; if you can't change it,
change the way you think about it.

Mary Engelbreit, artist

When problems arise, focus on solutions and moving
forward rather than dwelling on the issue and how it arose.

Go on a mass march, take part in peaceful protests,
write letters to express concerns, start local initiatives…
Whatever it is you feel strongly about, make an effort to
get your voice heard and you'll feel more positive about
the future, knowing that you're playing some small part in
helping to make things better.

33

travel

So often time it happens, we all live our lives in chains, and we never even know we have the key.

The Eagles

Even if it's just to a different part of town, travel somewhere. Engage in different cultures, or talk to new people. Take yourself away from your usual environment for a fresh perspective on life.

share your worries

The human spirit is stronger than anything that can
happen to it.

C. C. Scott, writer

You cannot do everything alone. Courage is not
plowing on unaided. It's braver to recognize your own
vulnerabilities, to acknowledge when you need help and to
seek it, let it happen and then give thanks for it.

Don't attempt to force positivity by repressing anything in
your life that's negative. This will have a detrimental effect
in the long run. Bring your problems out into the light by
sharing them with a trusted friend.

Visualize the negative thought and take the power away
from it by imagining it as a funny little creature. Describe it
to your friend and give it whatever amusing features your
imagination conjures up. Then finally give it wings and
watch it fly away together.

fake it till you make it

If you're walking down the right path and you're willing to
keep walking, eventually you'll make progress.

Barack Obama, 44th U.S. president

Act as if you're feeling positive, calm, decisive, or confident
and sure enough your mind will follow.

Whereas a certain amount of critical thinking is essential in
our decision-making processes, it's all too easy to over-think
situations when we're feeling less than brave about them.

However, once we start over-analysing, self-doubt creeps
in, we come up with an array of hypothetical negative
outcomes and we lose our confidence to go ahead.

Believe in yourself and take positive action before the fear
sets in. If it doesn't work out then chalk it up as experience
and embrace the lessons learned for next time.

test your resilience

If life throws stones at you, crush them and throw back glitter.

Terri Guillemets, writer

In order to remain hopeful even in times of turmoil, it's important to develop resilience. You need to learn how to function in distressing situations so consider practicing relaxation techniques, or call on friends who you consider part of your support system.

Recent studies suggest that resilience is actually something that can be learned. We all have times of stress or trauma in our lives. We can't stop these bad things from happening, but we can change how we react to them. Make the choice to respond in a way that protects your well-being.

Once you have developed strategies to encourage resilience, challenge yourself to remain positive even when things are going wrong. Can you pick yourself up and carry on? Of course you can.

make cuts from your life

It is your right to curate your life and your own perspective.

Lady Gaga, musician

To create space and time to invest energy in the things that you enjoy and the people you love, you may need to cull certain things from your life. Learn to say no to those things you do out of some misplaced sense of duty, and distance yourself from toxic friends who drain your reserves.

Declutter. We can all-too-easily accumulate too much "stuff". That "stuff" can become an overwhelming presence in our lives because it encroaches on our work or living space, or because we fret and worry about what to do with it. Take each item and consider its meaning or purpose in your life. If it is not of significant sentimental value or serving a practical purpose, consider donating it, gifting it or throwing it away. Creating a clutter-free space will create a calm and quiet environment and help you to attach positive feelings to everything within that space.

contemplate your values

We attract what we are prepared to receive.

Charles F. Glassman, motivational speaker

Knowing where your values lie will help you to make positive shifts in your life. For example, if you value time at home with your family more than anything, yet spend 90 percent of your time out at work, then you will constantly feel internally conflicted.

What really matters to you? What are your life values? Once you have defined these make a list of everything in your life that goes against them.

Living contrary to your values is a fast track to negativity and feelings of low self-worth. So today identify one thing you could do to make your life step back in line with your values.

make small, positive changes at home

The more you are positive and say "I want to have a good life", the more you build that reality for yourself by creating the life that you want.

Chris Pine, actor

Scatter plants throughout your living space, rearrange furniture, make your bed each morning, tidy up as you go along, string up some fairylights ... Adjusting small habits and routines around your home will have a positive impact on all areas of your life. It can help alleviate feelings of being stuck in a rut and will usher in a more positive energy.

reframe your challenges

Your attitude, not your aptitude, will determine your altitude.

Unknown

The most fearless people turn every obstacle they encounter into an opportunity. They are not daunted by challenges or put off course by disappointments and rejection. Try to see challenging events as gifts and utilize them to move forward. Rather than allowing them to stop you in your tracks, let them motivate you to try harder.

See each challenge as an opportunity for growth. Instead of feeling defeated by an obstacle, can you instead think about how overcoming it will help you develop as a person?

Treat every challenge as molehills not mountains and use your creativity and persistence to find solutions to overcome them.

forgive yourself

Instead of hating, I have chosen to forgive and spend all of my positive energy on changing the world.

Camryn Manheim, actress

Practicing self-compassion is an incredibly important component in developing emotional resilience, essential in developing the courage required to live a full life. So be kind to yourself. Do not punish yourself for being a flawed, imperfect human being. Recognize when you are being overly self-critical and replace those harsh words with kind, loving ones.

Instead of mourning past mistakes, forgive yourself and move on. Wallowing in regret won't help you.

42

embrace change

Life is made of peaks and troughs. If you don't like going up and down then you must live your life standing in one spot.

Alex Zar, politician and attorney

Don't let comfort cloud your judgement. Life can become stale if we stand still for too long. Embrace change and don't be afraid to step out of your comfort zone.

Routines can bring positive structure to our lives but sometimes we get stuck in ruts and find certain routines mundane. Our moods, creativity and motivation can be stifled by repetitive patterns and cycles, but changing your personal protocol can be hugely rewarding.

Try stepping out of your comfort zone in small ways every day. Change up your routine – walk to work instead of driving, get up earlier, take a different route home, start a conversation with a stranger ... Anything that goes slightly against the grain for you will force you into different situations. You will find yourself making braver and bolder choices, however minor, instead of running on autopilot.

cultivate optimism

The optimist proclaims that we live in the best of all possible worlds, and the pessimist fears this is true.

James Branch Cabell, author

While conventional wisdom suggests it's wise to expect the worst – that way you won't be disappointed when things go wrong and it'll be a pleasant surprise if things work out – much research has suggested that this isn't the most helpful attitude to adopt, that pessimism can undermine your performance creating a self-fulfilling prophecy.

No matter how bad things are, you can always focus on how to make things better. Believe that life will improve. All things pass.

set reminders

Only in the darkness can you see the stars.

Martin Luther King, Jr., minister and activist

Help keep positivity front and centre of your life by
scattering reminders throughout your home. Write your
favourite positive quotes on post-it notes and stick them to
your screen or on cupboard doors.

Set reminders on your phone's calendar to prompt you to
take a quiet moment for yourself, or to stand up and walk
mindfully for just a few minutes.

share positivity

Be the reason someone smiles today.

Unknown

Strive to be encouraging and supportive of others. Pay your friends compliments, tell a co-worker they've done a great job, tell your partner you love them…

Imagine becoming a role model for someone you care deeply about. Picture them copying your every move. Would you want them to remain unfulfilled and static in their life, or would you prefer they had the courage to go out and chase their dreams?

the consequences of
negative thinking

**You have absolute control over but one thing, and that
is your thoughts.**

Napolean Hill, author

If you can recognize the circumstances that make you
doubt yourself, you can be proactive in removing yourself
from those situations.

Note down the scenarios that trigger self-doubt. Perhaps
it's talking to a particular family member or colleague that
always leaves you feeling negative and questioning your
own decisions, attending a certain meeting at work, or
engaging in particular activities ... Whatever it is that fuels
your self-doubt and resistance to move forward, raise your
self-awareness of it so next time you can act against and in
spite of it.

Make a list of the ways in which negative thinking affects
your life: how it impacts your relationships, your work, and
your emotional well-being. How could being more positive
change this?

understand your
emotions

The more clearly you understand yourself and your emotions,
the more you become a lover of what is.

Baruch Spinoza, philosopher

Learning to harness your emotions is a huge step in
cultivating positivity. When focused, emotions can be used
to spur you into action. Anger, for example, leaves no room
for fear and can really help to motivate you. There is a fine
balance to be struck here – too much anger can cloud your
thoughts and judgements; just enough and it can become a
valuable tool.

If you are afraid to do something, ask yourself why.
Challenge yourself by asking the following questions:

•What am I actually afraid of?
•How could this action harm me or anyone else?
•What could happen as a result of my action?

By evaluating your emotions in this way you are more
likely to act rationally and positively rather than based on
an initial, negative emotional response.

embrace mother nature

Dwell on the beauty of life. Watch the stars, and see yourself running with them.

Marcus Aurelius, Roman emperor

There's a lot to be said for making believe everything's rosy. Spend some time in nature and notice the beauty in the world. Put on your rose-tinted spectacles and look for the best in everything and you'll soon start to see life as an adventure rather than a series of challenges.

Exposure to sunlight releases feel-good chemicals in our brains, immediately enhancing our mood. Try to get outside and soak up the rays, weather permitting, for at least 20 minutes a day.

Take a walk in the woods, swim in a lake, or simply stroll around your garden feeling the earth at your feet and the quality of the outside air fill your lungs. Relish the sun on your face or the rain cleansing your skin, the gentle breeze or refreshing gusts, star-laden skies or billowing clouds.

take the lead

Positive thinking will let you do everything better than
negative thinking will.

Zig Ziglar, author and motivational speaker

Remember you are in charge of your thoughts, not the
other way around. Take control and direct your thoughts
to positive places whenever possible.

If you don't achieve a goal, tell yourself you will get closer
next time. If someone criticizes you, instead of taking it
to heart, take it as an opportunity to improve. If someone
does better than you, learn from them. Take every
setback as an opportunity for growth and have faith in
your potential.

50

Many of us suppress our feelings in order to keep the
peace with others. This is so restrictive and can lead to
a mediocre existence. Have the strength to express your
feelings and take control of situations that may arise.
Have the courage to live the life you want to.

ban the word "can't"

Limit your "always" and your "nevers".

Amy Poehler, actress and comedian

Use only positive language and see how the mind follows. Instead of claiming you can't do something, vow to just try your best.

According to a Stanford Research Institute study, a positive and optimistic attitude contributes to success in life more than anything else. It suggests that 87.5 percent of people's success can be traced to their can-do and positive attitudes, while just 12.5 percent of their success comes from their aptitude, knowledge or skills.

see the best in yourself

A strong, positive self-image is the best-possible preparation
for success.

Joyce Brothers, psychologist and television personality

A fear of looking silly, inexperienced, weak or uneducated holds so many of us back. Today, let go of this fear of making a fool of yourself. Other people will have forgotten whatever foible you may or may not make long before you do.

Believe that you have a gift to offer, one that nobody else on earth can. Nobody brings to the table exactly what you do. Trust in the fact that you are the best candidate for that job, the perfect partner for somebody or the ideal business proposition…

52

Write a list of your best traits and keep it to hand for when self-esteem is low.

see the best in others

Start each day with a positive thought and a grateful heart.

Roy T. Bennett, writer and motivational speaker

Criticising other people is incredibly detrimental. This negativity will be a huge distraction from forging out the life you want to live and the world you want to live in.

For every negative thought you have about another person, remind yourself of two positive things about them, whether it's some small favour they've done for you or an admirable personality trait. Look hard enough for the best in those around you and sure enough you'll find it.

If another person is being rude and taking their bad mood out on you, try to respond with kindness and patience. Let their insults effortlessly roll off you and appreciate that the person doing you wrong is likely to be facing their own struggles. Don't let them drag you into their realm of negativity.

live in the now

Do not give your past the power to define your future.

Unknown

The only thing that truly exists is the present moment. Learn to embody it through breathing techniques. Simply stop whatever you are doing, close your eyes, and take three big belly breaths to feel instantly more grounded in the now.

Grounding yourself in the present moment in this way puts you into a state of focused flow. You are more likely to stop overthinking your situation and to just get on with whatever work needs doing. If you remind yourself that all you can do is your best right NOW you will be able to put all of your energies into the task at hand.

visualize success

Create the highest, grandest vision possible for your life,
because you become what you believe.

Oprah Winfrey, talk show host

Sometimes simply imagining a best-case outcome can help
bring it to fruition. Picture yourself having completed a
project or achieved a personal goal. Set the scene – what
does this look like? How do you feel?

Envisage your best self in the future. What are you doing?
Write about it in a journal to encourage and motivate you
to strive towards this outcome.

Write your own story – literally. Put pen to paper and
write what you would like to happen in your life right now.
Doing this can help to consolidate your ambitions and
hopes, as well as motivate you to make the story come true.

be playful

The person who can bring the spirit of laughter into a room
is indeed blessed.

Bennett Cerf, publisher and co-founder of Random House

As children we were unafraid to climb the tallest tree or
fling ourselves down treacherous slopes in a toboggan, yet
once we reach adulthood, life has taught us to be fearful of
many things.

The sensible "what if" part of our brain kicks in and
inhibits us in ways that it didn't when we were children.
Our knowledge of everything that could go wrong holds
us back. Try to embrace the Zen Buddhism concept of "a
beginner's mind" by adopting the enthusiastic, curious,
open mind of a child. Question what you would do if you
weren't afraid.

Lift your mood by indulging your inner child and having
a little fun. Play a silly game or spend time with children
who ignite the spirit of playfulness in you.

get inspired

Winners make a habit of manufacturing their own positive
expectations in advance of the event.

Brian Tracy, motivational speaker and self-development author

Read an autobiography of someone you admire, listen to
positivity podcasts or read blogs – gain inspiration from
others' achievements, or let positive outlooks influence
your own.

Perhaps you can find a mentor? Look amongst the
people you know for anyone who has faced adversity in
a courageous manner. Ask them how they made their
decisions, overcame their fears and confronted their
obstacles. Take as much advice as you can from the bravest
person in your life.

ignore the news

It is your responsibility to make sure that positive emotions
constitute the dominating influence of your mind.

Napolean Hill, author

Take a day off from watching the news and reading
newspapers. All too often we're fed depressing news and
brought stories of gloom that are bound to impact on even
the most optimistic among us. Limit your exposure to
avoid a spiralling descent into negative thought patterns.

Instead, cultivate a belief in humanity. Remember that
however dark and depressing a place the world can seem,
the light of humanity shines through it all. Read stories of
people who have made the world a brighter place in their
darkest hours to counterbalance the bad news that gets fed
to us daily.

practise positive affirmations

When we fill our thoughts with right things, the wrong ones have no room to enter.

Joyce Meyer, Christian author

Reminding yourself of all your positive attributes also makes them more likely to fire up when you need them, and reciting mantras can be a great way to train your brain to manifest positivity.

Identify the most positive aspects of your life, your strengths, your best character traits and values, and make a list of them. Then turn everything on that list into a positive statement. Try, for example, "I am happy", "I have all that I need", "My life is filled with joy", "I am loved."

Repeat these self-affirmations throughout the day and at any point when you find yourself overwhelmed with negative thoughts.

accept praise

There are exactly as many special occasions in life as we
choose to celebrate.

Robert Brault, writer

A huge part of becoming a more positive person lies
in accepting praise. When somebody praises you for
something, don't discredit them as is so often our natural
stock response. Instead, accept compliments with grace
and openness. Let other people's positive assessment of you
motivate you to succeed.

When you have succeeded in something or accomplished
a goal, tell people! We so often fall into the trap of only
talking to friends about what worries us and what we're
failing at. While this kind of support is vital, remember
to also seek feedback from friends and family to reinforce
the positive outcome of your actions. The more positive
feedback you get from those around you, the more inspired
and motivated you'll be to succeed again.

be authentic

Live your days on the positive side of life, in tune with your most treasured values. And in each moment you'll have much to live for.

Ralph Marston, American football player

Be true to yourself and your beliefs – and live in alignment with them – and you will naturally feel more positive about your life.

Don't be fooled into thinking that to be open-minded, a courageous risk taker and to embrace a full life you need to say yes to everything and everyone all of the time. Learning how to say no will help you to stay focused and prevent you from taking wrong turns or getting involved with the wrong people.

If you feel your life has meaning, and you are living your best life, it is much easier to live with hope in your heart. So how do you find your life's true purpose? One trick is to ask yourself what you would do with your life if you only had one year to live. Your answer will clarify what you truly value and therefore what you should be prioritizing.

take savasana

Occasionally it's good to pause, take a moment and remind yourself of the things in your life that are just fine.

Robert Brault, writer

Traditionally taken at the end of yoga sessions, Savasana (or Corpse Pose) is the ultimate surrender to gratitude. Lie on your back with your arms gently resting at your sides, feel the earth rise up to support you, and surrender your muscles into the ground or your yoga mat. In this resting position, find stillness. Give thanks for the air on your skin, to the earth supporting you, and feel your stress melt away.

avoid negative people

Surround yourself with people who make you hungry for life,
touch your heart, and nourish your soul.

Unknown

People who always expect the worst from life and who look
critically on all that surrounds them will inevitably drain
your energy. It's hard to retain positivity in an environment
imbued with criticism and pessimism.

listen to music

I've decided that the stuff falling through the cracks is confetti
and I'm having a party!

Betsy Cañas Garmon, writer and transition coach

Listening to any music that you enjoy can improve your
mood. Make it an upbeat tune for an extra burst of
positive energy.

Sing along. Sing loud. Sing with abandon and like no
one's listening.

Dance, too. Dance with carefree abandon and like no one's
watching. Dance until you're sweating. Dance until you
can't wipe the smile off your face.

64

choose joy

When it rains, it pours. You decide what comes down.

Justin Uyehara, businessman

Each day we wake up we can make the decision to be happy. We cannot decide what life will throw our way, but we can always make a choice as to how we react to it.

The happiest and most positive people do not seek happiness in other people or possessions. They are not held hostage by circumstance. They understand that joy and contentment comes from within and it is a choice. Today, whatever is going on in your life, choose happiness.

learn lessons

Be thankful for everything that happens in your life; it's all an experience.

Roy T. Bennett, writer and motivational speaker

Instead of berating yourself for past mistakes, think of the lessons you've learned along the way and how you can now apply this new wisdom to your life. This can quickly turn an attitude of defeat into one of optimism.

You are where you are in life because of the decisions and actions (or inaction) you have taken. At each stage in life you have made choices that have brought you here. By acknowledging your responsibility in this way you are empowering yourself to shape the future – in whatever way you choose.

accept yourself as you are

Whatever is, is best.

Ella Wheeler Wilcox, author and poet

Accept the things that you cannot change about yourself.
For example, if you're naturally an introvert you need
time alone to recharge your batteries so don't try and force
yourself to socialize all the time.

Have the conviction to tread your own path through
life, regardless of other people's expectations. Don't just
follow a certain direction in life because that's the natural
progression, and therefore what everyone will expect you
to do. You don't have to take the path of least resistance,
take the one less travelled if that one suits you better! Don't
be afraid to do the unexpected.

find the opportunity

Your hardest times often lead to the greatest moments of your life. Keep going. Tough situations build strong people in the end.

Roy T. Bennett, writer and motivational speaker

There's an opportunity to be found in even the most negative circumstances. Losing a job, for example, could provide you with just the push you need to take your career in another direction or start your own venture. The end of a relationship can bring precious alone time needed in order to grow as a person.

It's often in adversity that we come to realize our inner strength. Challenges in life will help you to develop characteristics you never knew you had, to connect to your inner core, and to therefore move forward with greater self-knowledge and renewed hope.

stand tall

Believe you can and you're halfway there.

Theodore Roosevelt, 26th U.S. President

Posture reflects your mindset – sitting slouched in a chair will make you look and feel defeated. On the other hand, walk tall with your head held high and you'll automatically feel more ready to take on the day.

Adjusting your posture can have a big effect on how confident and motivated you're feeling. If you can project the air of confidence you will subsequently start to feel it.

Try it for a day and see what a difference it makes; if you're sitting down, don't slouch but sit up straight with your shoulders back; walk with a determined stride and keep your head held high and your eyes on the horizon.

savour small pleasures

Think big thoughts but relish small pleasures.

H. Jackson Brown, Jr., author

Whether it's a cup of hot coffee, the smell of baking bread,
warming your toes by a roaring log fire, or basking in a
sunny spot in your backyard, savour all the small pleasures
that life offers up.

thank somebody

Choosing to be positive and having a grateful attitude is going to determine how you're going to live your life.

Joel Osteen, pastor

Take the time today to show your gratitude to someone. Perhaps a neighbour has done you a favour, a friend has been there for you in tough times, or you have neglected to show a parent how much you appreciate them.

Invite positivity into your life by sending text messages, emails, or letters of appreciation to friends and family – just a line to tell them how much you appreciate them and why. In turn, their responses will show you how much they care, too.

name your fears

To name your fears is to destroy them.

Unknown

Sometimes we can't quite pin down what it is that we're scared of and this uncertainty only increases anxiety. Find some time to sit in silence and engage in self-reflection to identify exactly what it is you're afraid of.

Write down a list of your fears. This can be difficult, it may make you feel embarrassed or ashamed, but persevere. Identifying, naming and admitting your fears is the first step in facing them.

Now visualize your fears as clouds floating across the sky. Label each "worry cloud" as it floats past without passing judgement. This is a really useful exercise in distancing yourself from your fears. It helps you to recognize them as something separate from yourself. Acknowledge the fact that they are removed from you, not a part of your being and as such they do not have to dictate your life.

take responsibility

A positive attitude is something everyone can work on, and everyone can learn how to employ it.

Joan Lunden, journalist and author

Only you have the power to live a positive and joyful life. Don't look to others to shift your mood or shape your mindset. The responsibility for your happiness is yours alone.

Trust in yourself and your own instincts. Don't shy away from defending your actions. Have conviction in your opinions and behaviour and don't let anybody talk you into or out of situations.

focus on fun

A good laugh is sunshine in the house.

William Makepeace Thackeray, author and illustrator

So often the responsibilities of life weigh us down and we spend our days devoted to our work or caring for others. We can all too easily forget what it is that we actually enjoy doing.

Every day try to steal a moment for yourself to do something alone you enjoy – reading a book with a glass of wine, listening to your favourite music track, savouring the perfect mug of coffee in silence. Realize that whatever is going on in your life, you can gift yourself one happy moment of peace each and every day.

Write down ten things you find fun and vow to do at least one of these every day.

don't live life through a screen

What consumes your mind controls your life.

Unknown

If you're at an event, watch it with your eyes, not through the filter of a screen. Fully embrace the good times and ground yourself in that moment. Stop worrying about trying to capture it on camera or post live feeds to showcase the highlights reel of your life.

practise asanas

When you listen to yourself, everything comes naturally. It comes from inside, like a kind of will to do something. Try to be sensitive. That is yoga.

Petri Räisänen, interantionally renowned Ashtanga yoga teacher

These are the physical postures of yoga, many of which promote a healthy flow of energy throughout the body, unite body and mind, and encourage feelings of joy. You don't need to be flexible or a seasoned yogi to engage in simple postures. Try Balasana (Child's Pose); a surrender to the earth and an invitation to spiral inward via the breath to find self-love and comfort. Or stand tall in Tadasana (Mountain Pose) to feel rooted to the earth and an indestructible positive energy.

76

focus on the "cans"

Virtually nothing is impossible in this world if you just put your mind to it and maintain a positive attitude.

Lou Holtz, former American football player and coach

Don't dwell on things you can't change, instead concentrate on everything you can do to make your world a little brighter.

Focusing on your flaws just taps into the mindset of fear and undermines your feelings of self-worth. There are always going to be some areas in which you're weaker than others but if you concentrate on these instead of your positive attributes you will end up feeling ashamed of yourself – an emotion not conducive to courageous actions.

If you are having a thought that undermines your attempt at positivity, simply notice it and tell yourself "oh there's a fearful thought." By paying attention to your thoughts and labelling them in this non-judgemental, conscious way you are distancing yourself from the thought itself and as such are far less likely to let it influence your behaviour.

explore and learn

Look at everything as though you were seeing it either for the
first or last time.

Betty Smith, author

Explore new places, search your mind for avenues of
potential new interest. Listen to other people's ideas
and opinions. Be curious about the people and things
around you.

If you are hesitant about a situation, get informed. Ask
lots of questions or make sure you do your research.
Remember that ignorance can contribute to worsening our
fears. As we learn more about a situation, a person or an
event then the fear surrounding them is likely to dissipate.
Often it's the uncertainty that holds us back.

focus on what
you can control

I am not a product of my circumstances. I am a product of my decisions.

Stephen R. Covey, educator and author

It's hard to act courageously when you're feeling out of control. Yet you will never have control over everything – you can control your actions, yet you have no control over the results of these. So focus on your actions and behaviour, not the outcome.

So much of life is beyond our control but rather than ruminating on this, focus instead on the things you can control. For example, you can't control being made redundant from your job, but you can control how you go about looking for your next job. You can't control a medical diagnosis, but you can take steps to take care of yourself through good nutrition and rest.

make positive
thinking a habit

Every thought is a seed. If you plant crab apples, don't count
on harvesting Golden Delicious.

Bill Meyer, artist

Whatever your mood, actively train your brain to think
and see the positive in every situation. Think of this as a
preventative measure – don't wait until you're feeling down
to engage in positive thinking.

Self-doubt is fuelled by disastrous predictions – often ones
that have no grounding in reality. So if you find yourself
struggling against a positive outlook, ask yourself what's
the worst that could happen.

Consider the worst-case scenario and most likely you will
realize that even if things go wrong, events are unlikely to
be life altering. Keep things in perspective and don't let
unfounded worries hold you back.

believe in yourself

If you have a positive attitude and constantly strive to give your best effort, eventually you will overcome your immediate problems and find you are ready for greater challenges.

Pat Riley, former basketball coat and NBA player

Know that you have the strength within you to succeed at whatever you put your mind to. Believing you can achieve your goals will take you one step closer to doing just that.

If you repeatedly visualize yourself successfully carrying out a fearful task with confidence, your subconscious mind will come to accept these visions as instructions for the task. Feed your mind with positive mental images of yourself acting with competence and courage, and they may just become reality.

eat well

One cannot think well, love well, sleep well, if one has not dined well.

Virginia Woolf, writer

Eating a good, nutritious meal is an enjoyable activity in itself, but it can also seriously improve your psychological outlook. A lack of certain vitamins can impact on mental health, potentially leading to stress, anxiety, and other disorders. Try to eat well each day to help nurture a positive mindset.

reminisce

If you want to keep your memories, your first have to
live them.

Bob Dylan, musician

Look back on good times and contemplate how they made
you feel. Close your eyes and imagine being back in that
time and place. Relish the feelings that this evokes and
remind yourself that, just as there once were good times, so
will there be again.

Bring to mind all the times in your life when you have
acted positively, when you faced your fears and took a
leap into the unknown with successful outcomes.
Close your eyes and focus on how that made you feel.
Let these feelings inspire you to once again act with
positive intentions.

83

perform an act
of kindness

The thing that lies at the foundation of positive change, the
way I see it, is service to a fellow human being.

Lee Iacocca, automobile executive

Authentic happiness comes from helping others, plus it can
help you find meaning in your own life. So take some time
to focus outward on others around you. What can you do
today to help someone? Offer to help a friend or neighbour
in need and know that your kindness has started a ripple
effect of positivity.

Stand up for others. If you're in a situation where people
are gossiping unkindly about somebody, or someone in a
vulnerable position is being talked down to, speak out for
them. Feel your confidence grow as you become the voice
for someone who is being treated unfairly.

ditch perfection

If I waited for perfection, I would never write a word.

Margaret Atwood, writer

The quest for perfection is so often what stops us in our tracks before we've even begun. We're afraid that we can't do something perfectly and so we don't even try. Studies have shown that perfectionists actually tend to be less successful people than those who accept setbacks and learn from them. So today let go of the desire to be perfect and do everything perfectly – it will only ever impede your progress.

If you're feeling too scared to take the first step towards a new direction in life, is it because you are comparing yourself to others? That you're not as strong, intelligent, beautiful, deserving, confident, skilled or outgoing as them? Remember that everyone, even the most together-seeming people have their struggles. We're all just trying to find our way in an imperfect world.

reframe your days

The sun himself is weak when he first rises, and gathers
strength and courage as the day gets on.

Charles Dickens, Victorian novelist

Framing is a behavioural technique used to shape how
you think and feel about a situation. It's basically a way
of relabelling whatever it is that is making you feel sad
or anxious. If, for example, you're worried about an
upcoming exam, reframe it as a "quiz", a job interview
could become a "chat", a run can become a "jog".

Instead of seeing Monday as the day you have to drag
yourself out of bed, view it as a fresh start. The first day
of the week is a chance to begin again – list all of the
things you'd like to achieve that week and make Monday
a motivational day. Use the energy lag you experience on
a Wednesday to indulge in self-reflection and self-care,
make Thursday the day you try something new instead of
wishing the nearly-completed week away…

Each day is an opportunity to embrace positivity.

make peace with the past

The best is yet to be.

Robert Browning, poet and playwright

According to a rapidly growing body of research, holding a grudge and nursing grievances can affect physical as well as mental health. So learn how to forgive. Try to let go of past hurts. Move on with compassion in your heart and your head held high.

Living in the past will hinder your happiness in the present. If you need to address any issues or people to get closure, then do so. Then promise yourself not to go backwards again.

don't judge

Never limit yourself because of others' limited imagination;
never limit others because of your own limited imagination.

Mae Jemison, engineer and former NASA astronaut

Don't judge yourself too harshly. Allow yourself room to be
human and make mistakes, and make the same allowances
for other people. Start each day from a non-judgemental
place of quiet acceptance and see how this attitude
positively impacts every area of your life.

You can recognize all the bad things in your life and yet
choose to see all the good things, too. Remember your life
doesn't have to be perfect for you to be a positive person.

compliment yourself

You are enough just as you are.

Meghan Markle, Duchess of Sussex

We're constantly bombarded by messages and advertising that tells us a myriad of ways we can improve ourselves – get thinner, richer, smarter … Remind yourself you're fine just the way you are.

Repeat the mantra "I am worthy" on a daily basis. Make the effort to pay yourself a compliment each day and watch how your self-esteem improves.

Use the mirror method. Every morning stand in front of the mirror and list three things you like about yourself. You may feel self-conscious at first, but this is a great technique for building confidence and promoting a positive self-image.

start your day in
a positive way

**You're off to great places, today is your day. Your mountain is
waiting, so get on your way.**

Dr. Seuss, author and illustrator

The manner in which you spend your morning sets the
tone for the rest of your day. Instead of reaching for the
snooze button, switch your morning habits to something
more positive. Try a sun salutation, go for a jog, or simply
take a cup of coffee out to a sunny spot in your garden.

plan things to look forward to

If you want light to come into your life, you need to stand where it is shining.

Guy Finley, writer

Countless studies have shown that happiness fuels success and performance, not the other way around. You need to create a life around what makes you happy in order to fulfill your potential.

There are inevitably difficult or mundane periods in life when it's hard to attain or maintain a positive outlook. At times like this, plan some events that you can look forward to. Whether it's a weekend away with friends, a trip to visit family, or a meal in your favourite restaurant, schedule in things that will keep your mood buoyant through even the dreariest of days.

practise self-care

Take time to do what makes your soul happy.

Unknown

There's nothing like indulging in a little self-care to improve your mindset. Run yourself a hot bath, buy yourself flowers, curl up with a super soft blanket and a good book…

The mind–body link is unavoidable – it's impossible to have a healthy mind, to feel truly positive, if you're not looking after your body. So get moving! Exercise regularly to improve your fitness and increase endorphins and you'll feel more energized and hopeful.

take time out

There is virtue in work and there is virtue in rest. Use both
and overlook neither.

Alan Cohen, author

It may feel counterintuitive to just stop what you're doing
when you're aiming high, but in order to maintain a
motivated and positive mindset, that is exactly what you
need to do. If you are constantly exhausted and stressed it's
pretty much impossible to be confident and courageous in
the pursuit of your goals, so take time out for relaxation.
Spend 30 minutes each day walking, reading a book,
listening to music or chatting with friends ... Whatever
it is that helps you to relax, and watch your motivation
levels soar.

Try not to bring work home with you. Blurring the lines
between your work and home life can have a negative
impact on your mindset as well as eat into what could be
precious quality time with loved ones.

find your intrinsic motivation

Keep looking where the light pours in.

Morgan Harper Nichols, artist and writer

You are the controller of your own destiny, and while it's important to seek support from loved ones, it should not be their validation that you wait on to push you forward. For success to have longevity, your motivation has to be intrinsic, i.e. come from within, so look inside yourself, not outwardly to others, to find the strength you need to pursue your goals and dreams.

What motivates you intrinsically? In other words, what tasks do you enjoy doing just for the joy of doing them, regardless of the results or an end product. For example, do you find painting gives you a sense of peace regardless of what your finished picture looks like? The more you can indulge in such activities the more energized and fulfilled you'll feel.

don't compare

It's a funny thing about life, once you begin to take note of the things you are grateful for, you begin to lose sight of the things that you lack.

Germany Kent, journalist

Many of us spend too much time and energy worrying about what other people will think of us. What if we don't succeed in what we set out to achieve? What will people think? The truth is, very little. People are too busy in their own heads, consumed by their own thoughts, ideas, hopes, insecurities, dreams and failures to put yours under the microscope.

If you start to compare yourself to others, you will inevitably get caught in a spiral of negativity – there will always be someone somewhere who you judge to be doing things better than you. Don't look to what others have or are doing as a marker of your own success.

give unconditionally

In every day, there are 1,440 minutes. That means we have 1,440 daily opportunities to make a positive impact.

Les Brown, motivational speaker

Whether it's your time, material resources, or your love, this is probably the most emotionally uplifting act of all.

Keep on reminding yourself that generosity is not a transaction, and that just because someone hasn't shown kindness to you does not mean you cannot show kindness to them.

Giving unconditionally will boost your positive energy, and help you live a happier, more fulfilled life.